2

Fly High

Fun Grammar

Katerina Stavridou

 # Contents

Unit	Language	Page
Welcome to our zoo!		4
Alphabet, colours and numbers		6
Unit 1	*What's this? It's a/an …*	8
	a/an, The	9
	What are they? They're … Regular plurals	10
	This is/That is …	11
Fun Grammar Review 1		12
Unit 2	*be: Yes/No* questions *I/You/He/She/It*	14
	We/You/They	16
Fun Grammar Review 2		18
Unit 3	Possessive adjectives: *my, your, his, her, its, our, your, their*	20
Unit 4	*have got/has got:* affirmative and negative	22
	Yes/No questions	24
Fun Grammar Review 3		26
Unit 5	*There is/There are …*	28
	Where is/Where are …? Prepositions of place	30
Unit 6	*can:* affirmative and negative	32
	Yes/No questions	34
Fun Grammar Review 4		36
Unit 7	Present simple: affirmative and negative: *I/You/We/They*	38
	Yes/No questions: *Do you like …?*	40
	Affirmative: *He/She/It*	42
	Yes/No questions: *Does he swim every day?*	44
Fun Grammar Review 5		46

Unit	Language	Page
Unit 8	Present continuous: affirmative	48
	Negative	52
	Yes/No questions	54
Fun Grammar Review 6		56
Unit 9	*This is/These are …*	58
Unit 10	Irregular plurals: + *-es, y ⟶ -ies*, irregular forms	60
Unit 11	*some/any*	62
Unit 12	*Wh-* questions: *What, Who, Where, How many?*	65
Fun Grammar Review 7		68
I can do this! 1		70
I can do this! 2		72
I can do this! 3		74
Look what I can do!		76

Welcome to our zoo!

1 Write.

Hello............! ....Anna.
What's..............................?

.... Tom.

2 Write about you. Then draw.

Hi! I'm Tag. What's your name?

Hello! ....

3 Listen and write. Track 3

My name's Trumpet, how are you?
I'm an elephant in the zoo.
My (**1**) ....*name's*.... Chatter, how are you?
I'm a monkey in the zoo.
My name's Karla, (**2**) .... are you?
I'm a kangaroo in the zoo.
My name's Patty, how are you?
(**3**) .... a penguin in the zoo.
My name's Tag, how are you?
I'm a tiger in the zoo.
My name's Sally, how
(**4**) .... you?
I'm a keeper in the zoo.

How are you?
I'm fine, thank you.
We (**5**) .... the zoo!

Alphabet, colours and numbers

1 **Write.**

A → *a*

b → *B*

C → *c*

d → *D*

E → *e*

f → *F*

G → *g*

h → *H*

I → *i*

j → *J*

K → *k*

l → *L*

M → *m*

n → *N*

O → *o*

p → *P*

Q → *q*

r → *R*

S → *s*

t → *T*

U → *u*

v → *V*

W → *w*

X → *X*

Y → *y*

Z → *Z*

2 Circle the animals.

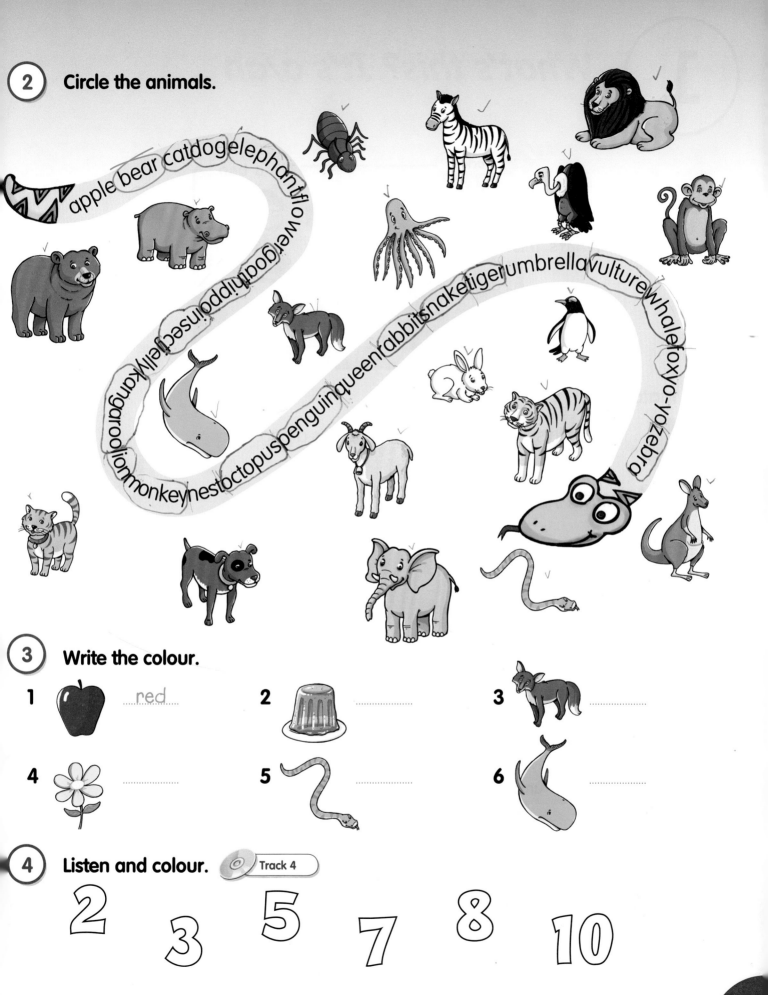

applebearcatdogelephantflowergoathippoinsectjellykangaroolionmonkeynestoctopuspenguinqueenrabbitsnaketigerumbrellavulturewhalefoxyo-yozebra

3 Write the colour.

1   red

2

3

4

5

6

4 Listen and colour.   Track 4

2   3   5   7   8   10

What's this? It's a/an ...

Track 5

What's this?

It's a bag.

1 **Match.**

1  What's this?

2 What's this?

3 What's this?

4 What's this?

5 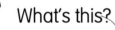 What's this?

a It's a bag.

b It's a rubber.

c It's a book.

d It's a pencil.

e It's a pen.

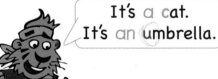

It's a cat.
It's an umbrella.

Track 6

Consonants: b c d f g h j k l m n p q r s t v w x y z
Vowels: a e i o u

We use a before consonants: a cat, a bag,
   a pen
We use an before vowels: an umbrella,
   an apple

a/an, The

2 **Write.**

1 It's ___a___ ___t___iger.

2 It's ___an___ ___e___lephant.

3 It's ___a___ ___C___at.

4 It's ___a___ ___m___onkey.

 Track 7

It's an octopus.
The octopus is purple.

It's an apple.
The apple is red.

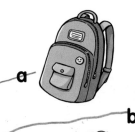

3 **Write and match.**

1 It's ___a___ pen. ___The___ pen is blue.

2 It's ___a___ bag. ___The___ bag is pink.

3 It's ___an___ elephant. ___The___ elephant is grey.

a

b

c

Let's Chat Track 8

What's this?

It's a cat.

This is a dog
These are dogs

1 What are they? They're ...
Regular plurals

One car.
Two flowers.

Track 9

Singular	Plural (+s)
a ball	two balls
a book	three books
a crayon	four crayons
a sticker	five stickers

4 Write.

1 What are they?
They're pens.

2 What are they?
They're stickers.

3  What are they?
They're chairs

4  What are they?
They're dolls.

 # Let's Sing Track 10

Listen and write.

cars ~~Orange~~ yellow pink Dolls

(**1**) Orange cars and (**2**) .... cars.
Cars for me and you!
One, two, three, four.
Lots of (**3**) ....
Cars for me and you.

Purple dolls and big, (**4**) .... dolls.
Dolls for me and you!
One, two, three, four.
Lots of dolls.
(**5**) .... for me and you.

This is/That is ...

That is **a cake.**

This is **a present.**

  Track 11

We use This is to talk about something near. We can touch it.

We use That is to talk about something far. We can point to it.

5 **Write** This is **or** That is.

1 What's this?	This is	a chair.
2 What's that?		a car.
3 What's this?		a watch.
4 What's that?		a card.

Let's Play

This is Sally.
That is Karla.

Fun Grammar Review 1

1 Listen and circle.  Track 12

1 a  b    2 a  b

3 a  b    4 a  b

5 a  b    6 a  b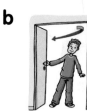

2 Circle.

1 It's .... book.
  a an   **b** a   **c** the

2 It's .... octopus. The octopus is purple.
  a a   **b** an   **c** the

3 It's a bag. .... bag is blue.
  a The   **b** An   **c** A

4 It's an apple. .... apple is red.
  a A   **b** An   **c** The

3 Match.

1 This is a book.

2 That is a robot.

3 This is a cake.

4 That is a present.

a

b

c

d

4 **Write** What's this **or** What are they.

1 ....**What's this**.... ? — It's a card.

2 .... ? — It's a rubber.

3 .... ? — They're stickers.

4 .... ? — It's a present.

My English

Write and draw. Then colour.

What's this? — It's a car. The car is orange.

What's _this_ ?
It's _a tank. The tank is green._

Now draw a face.

2 be: Yes/No questions
I/You/He/She/It

I am

I'm Tag. You're Patty.

She is

She's Sally.

He is

He's Trumpet.

It is

Track 13

We use He for a boy or a man.

We use She for a girl or a woman.

We use It for things.

When we speak, we use short forms:

Affirmative		Negative	
Long forms	**Short forms**	**Long forms**	**Short forms**
I am	I'm	I am not	I'm not
You are	You're	You are not	You aren't
He is	He's	He is not	He isn't
She is	She's	She is not	She isn't
It is	It's	It is not	It isn't

1 Circle.

1 I'm Tag.
   a 'm   **b** 's

2 You _aren't_ Sally.
   a aren't   **b** 'm not

3 He _is not_ my dad.
   a isn't   **b** aren't

4 It 's a book.
   a 're   **b** 's

5 She 's my sister.
   a 'm   **b** 's

6 I _'m not_ a teacher.
   a 'm not   **b** isn't

Is he a boy?

Yes, he is!

Questions	Short answers
Am I …?	Yes, you are./No, you aren't.
Are you …?	Yes, I am./No, I'm not.
Is he …?	Yes, he is./No, he isn't.
Is she …?	Yes, she is./No, she isn't.
Is it …?	Yes, it is./No, it isn't.

We use short forms to answer No:
   No, I'm not.   No, you aren't.
But we use long forms to answer Yes:
   Yes, I am. ✔   ~~Yes, I'm.~~ ✗
   Yes, you are. ✔   ~~Yes, you're.~~ ✗

(2) **Circle.**

1 Is he a boy? (Yes, he is.) / No, she isn't.   **2** Are you a teacher? Yes, it is. / No, I'm not.
3 Is she a girl? Yes, she is. / No, he isn't.   **4** Is it a goat?   Yes, I am. / No, it isn't.

(3) **Write** Are **or** Is**. Then answer.**

1 __Is__ (she) your mum? Yes, __she is__ .

2 .... you a girl? No, ...

3 .... she your sister? No, ...

4 .... you a girl? Yes, ...

5 .... (he) your grandpa? No, ...

6 .... it a baby? Yes, ...

Let's Chat   Track 15

 Are you a boy?

 Yes, I am.

2 We/You/They

We're dancers.

They're cowboys.

Affirmative		Negative	
Long forms	**Short forms**	**Long forms**	**Short forms**
We are	We're	We are not	We aren't
You are	You're	You are not	You aren't
They are	They're	They are not	They aren't

4 Match.

a

c

1 You're cowboys.

2 They're teachers.

3 They're boys.

4 We're friends.

b

d

5 Write the short forms.

1 You are cowboys.   You're cowboys.
2 We are dancers.   .... dancers.
3 They are not dancers.   .... dancers.
4 You are not teachers.   .... teachers.

Are they pirates?

No, they aren't.

Track 17

Questions	Short answers
Are we …?	Yes, you are./No, you aren't.
Are you …?	Yes, we are./No, we aren't.
Are they …?	Yes, they are./No, they aren't.

(6) Write.

1 ....Are they.... clowns? Yes, they are.

2 .... kings? No, we aren't.

3 .... dancers? Yes, you are.

4 .... queens? No, they aren't.

Let's Sing **Track 18**

Listen and put a ✓.

❶  ✓   ❷  □   ❸  □   ❹   □

❺   □   ❻  □   ❼   □   ❽   □

Fun Grammar Review ②

1 Listen and write. Track 19

........Tom........

....

2 Circle.

1 He ...... my grandpa.
  a 'm   **b** 's   **c** 're

2 I ...... a clown.
  a 's   **b** 're   **c** 'm

3 They ...... pirates.
  a 're   **b** 's   **c** 'm

4 You ...... my friend.
  a 'm   **b** 're   **c** 's

3 Match.

1 Is he a king?
2 Are you a teacher?
3 Are they cowboys?
4 Is she a dancer?
5 Is it a crown?

a Yes, they are.
b Yes, it is.
c No, I'm not.
d Yes, he is.
e No, she isn't.

4 Write.

1 She ....*is*.... my mum.
3 They .... girls.
5 I .... happy.

2 .... he your dad?
4 .... you a baby?
6 .... she your grandma?

5 Write.

1  She is a queen.

2 He is king

3   They gre cloicn3

4 It iz a box

5  we are pirates

6  i am a cowboy

My English

Write and draw. Then colour.

 This is my friend.
He's John. He's a boy.
He's eight. He's happy.

 This is ....
....
....

Now draw a face.

3 Possessive adjectives:
my, your, his, her, its, our, your, their

> I'm Sally. This is my radio.
> She is Karla. That is her doll.

Track 20

Personal pronouns	Possessive adjectives
I	my
you	your
he	his
she	her
it	its
we	our
you	your
they	their

We always use a noun after a possessive adjective.

   This is my radio. My radio is red.

   That is her ball. Her ball is blue.

1 Circle.

1 I'm Chatter. This is .... kite.

  a my   **b** her

2 He's my brother. .... book is new.

  a His   **b** Their

3 She's my mum. .... car is small.

  a His   **b** Her

4 We're the winners. This is .... prize.

  a my   **b** our

5 It's my doll. .... clothes are green.

  a Our   **b** Its

6 You're my friend. They're .... toys.

  a your   **b** its

2 **Match and write.**

1  He's Tag.
That's .....his..... bike.

a

2  She's Karla.
That's .... doll.

b

3  They're Patty and Trumpet.
That's .... train.

c

4  I'm Chatter.
That's .... computer game.

d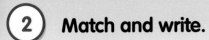

Let's Play

This is Tag.
His bike is orange.

Yes!

4 have got / has got:
affirmative and negative

I've got small feet.
She's got big feet.

I haven't got small feet.

Track 21

Affirmative		Negative	
Long forms	**Short forms**	**Long forms**	**Short forms**
I have got	I've got	I have not got	I haven't got
You have got	You've got	You have not got	You haven't got
He has got	He's got	He has not got	He hasn't got
She has got	She's got	She has not got	She hasn't got
It has got	It's got	It has not got	It hasn't got
We have got	We've got	We have not got	We haven't got
You have got	You've got	You have not got	You haven't got
They have got	They've got	They have not got	They haven't got

1 Match.

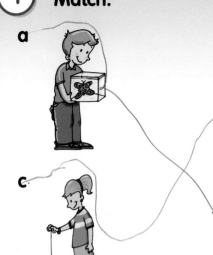

a

1 I've got a dog.

2 She's got a yo-yo.

3 They haven't got a small present.

4 He's got a pet.

b

d

c

2 Circle.

1 They .... six legs.
  (a) haven't got   b hasn't got

2 They .... a car.
  (a) haven't got   b hasn't got

3 It .... wings.
  (a) has got   b have got

4 We .... rollerblades.
  a has got   **(b)** have got

5 She .... a bag.
  a haven't got   **(b)** hasn't got

6 I .... three arms.
  (a) haven't got   b hasn't got

3 Write.

Long forms

1 I _have got_ two legs.
2 They _have got_ big feet.
3 She _has got_ small hands.

Short forms

I _'ve got_ two legs.
They _have got_ big feet.
She _'s got_ small hands.

4 Write.

Long forms

1 He _has not got_ a fast car.
2 We _have not got_ two books.
3 It _has not got_ two wings.

Short forms

He _hasn't got_ a fast car.
We _haven't got_ two books.
It _hasn't got_ two wings.

4 Yes/No questions

Have you got big feet?

No, I haven't.

Track 22

Questions	Short answers
Have I got …?	Yes, you have./No, you haven't.
Have you got …?	Yes, I have./No, I haven't.
Has he got …?	Yes, he has./No, he hasn't.
Has she got …?	Yes, she has./No, she hasn't.
Has it got …?	Yes, it has./No, it hasn't.
Have we got …?	Yes, you have./No, you haven't.
Have you got …?	Yes, we have./No, we haven't.
Have they got …?	Yes, they have./No, they haven't.

5 Circle.

1 Has she got long brown hair?
Yes, she has. / No, she hasn't.

2 Has she got a small nose?
Yes, she has. / No, she hasn't.

3 Has she got blue eyes?
Yes, she has. / No, she hasn't.

4 Has he got brown eyes?
Yes, he has. / No, he hasn't.

5 Has he got short brown hair?
Yes, he has. / No, he hasn't.

6 Has he got a big nose?
Yes, he has. / No, he hasn't.

6 **Write** Have **or** Has**. Then match.**

1 _Have_ you got an insect?   Yes, it has.

2 .... it got six legs?   No, she hasn't.

3 .... butterflies got arms?   Yes, I have.

4 .... Karla got small feet?   Yes, they have.

5 .... Tag got small feet?   No, they haven't.

6 .... elephants got big ears?   Yes, he has.

7 **Write in the correct order.**

1 you / Have / a sister? / got   _Have you got a sister?_

2 Has / a pet? / got / he   ....

3 got / They've / a car.   ....

4 a cat. / got / I've   ....

Let's Sing  Track 23

Listen and circle.

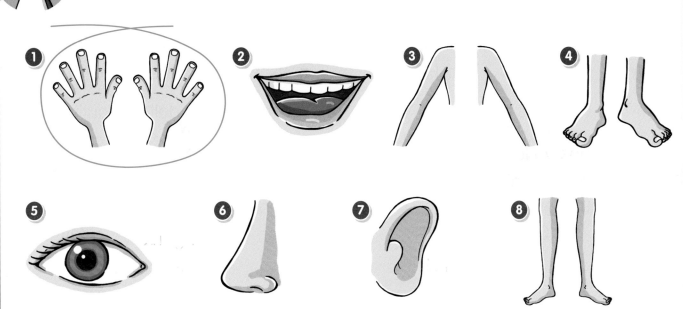

Fun Grammar Review 3

1 Put a ✓ or a ✗.

1 This is my bike. ✓

2 This is his book. _____

3 This is Amy. Her radio is red. _____

4 They're our rollerblades. _____

2 Circle.

1 She's my mum. ...... car is slow.
  a My **b** Her **c** His

2 This is my pet. ...... wings are long.
  a Its **b** His **c** Our

3 I'm Tom. ...... kite is blue.
  a My **b** Its **c** Their

4 You're a girl. ...... doll is beautiful.
  a His **b** Her **c** Your

5 He's my brother John.
...... computer game is old.
  a My **b** Her **c** His

6 They're my friends. ...... school
is small.
  a Her **b** Their **c** My

3 Look and write.

Joe | Anna | Tina | Bob

1 Joe ___has got a car___ . ___He hasn't got___ a train.

2 Tina _____ . _____ a car.

3 Anna _____ . _____ a kite.

4 Bob _____ . _____ a doll.

4 Write Have or Has. Then answer.

1 ___Has___ she got a doll? Yes, ___she has___ .

2 _____ he got a bike? No, _____ .

3 _____ they got a box? No, _____ .

4 _____ you got a train? Yes, _____ .

5 _____ she got a computer game? No, _____ .

My English

Write about your friend.

My friend, Mary, has got brown hair and black eyes. She's got a pet. Her dog is small and brown. Its name is Max.

My friend, _____

_____ .

_____

_____

Now draw a face.

5 There is/There are ...

> There's a river.
> There are lots of trees.

Track 24

Singular

Long forms

There is a flower.

There is a duck.

Short forms

There's a flower.

There's a duck.

Plural

There are flowers.

There are ducks.

There are has no short form.

---

1 **Choose and write.**

four children   trees   a park   a swimming pool   a house   lots of animals

an apple   two cats

There is	There are
a park	

(2) **Write** There's **or** There are.

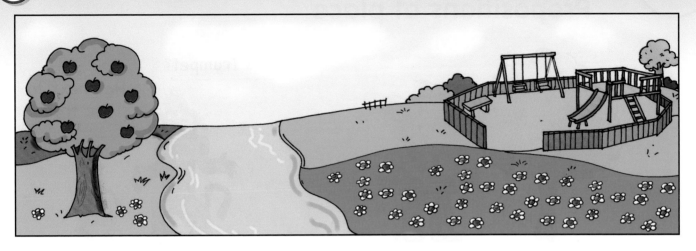

(1) ⟨There's⟩ a park in my town. **(2)** _____ a playground.

(3) _____ a tree. **(4)** _____ lots of apples. **(5)** _____ lots

of flowers too. **(6)** _____ a river.

Let's Sing  Track 25

Listen and write.

There   ~~tigers~~   hippos   animals   monkeys   penguins

There are lots of animals in our zoo.
Lions, **(1)** ⟨tigers⟩ and kangaroos.
Bears and **(2)** _____ and
zebras too.
We love the **(3)** _____ and they
love you.

(4) _____ are lots of animals in
our zoo.
Snakes, **(5)** _____ and cockatoos.
Goats and **(6)** _____ and
elephants too.
We love the animals and they love you.

Where is/Where are …?
Prepositions of place

Where's Trumpet?

He's next to the tree.

Track 26

Singular		**Plural**
Long form	**Short form**	Where are the cats?
Where is the cat?	Where's the cat?	

Where are has no short form.

You can use prepositions of place to answer questions with Where.

in   on   under   next to

Where's the dog? It's under the climbing frame.

3 **Circle.**

1 ...... the girls?

   a Where's   **(b)** Where are

2 ...... the children?

   a Where's   **b** Where are

3 ...... the shop?

   a Where's   **b** Where are

4 ...... Sally and Patty?

   a Where's   **b** Where are

5 ...... the swing?

   a Where's   **b** Where are

6 ...... the zoo?

   a Where's   **b** Where are

4 Put a ✓ or a ✗.

1 Tag is on the climbing frame. ✓
2 Trumpet is under the slide. ....
3 Patty is on the swing. ....
4 Sally is in the treehouse. ....
5 Karla is next to Vicky. ....

5 Write.

1 It's .... on the slide ....   2 It's ....

3 It's ....   4 It's ....

Let's Chat Track 27

Where's Sally?

She's in the shop.

6 can: affirmative and negative

I can ride a bike.

Track 28

Can is the same with all personal pronouns.

I/You/He/She/It/We/They can jump.

1 Match.

1 She can swim.

2 He can play the guitar.

3 I can jump.

4 We can dance.

a

b

c

d

2 Write.

1
She can
play the guitar.

2
run fast.

3
climb a tree.

4
fly high.

The negative of can is cannot. The short form is can't.

I/You/He/She/It/We/They cannot/can't sing.

---

(3) **Circle.**

1 Tigers can / can't climb.

2 Snakes can / can't run.

3 Penguins can / can't walk.

4 Elephants can / can't fly.

5 Hippos can / can't sing.

6 Monkeys can / can't jump.

(4) **Write about you.**

1 .... swim.

2 .... climb.

3 .... play the guitar.

4 .... rollerblade.

5 .... do a handstand.

6 .... fly.

6 Yes/No questions

Can you rollerblade?

Yes, I can.

Track 30

Questions	Short answers
Can I …?	Yes, you can./No, you can't.
Can you …?	Yes, I can./No, I can't.
Can he …?	Yes, he can./No, he can't.
Can she …?	Yes, she can./No, she can't.
Can it …?	Yes, it can./No, it can't.
Can we …?	Yes, you can./No, you can't.
Can you …?	Yes, we can./No, we can't.
Can they …?	Yes, they can./No, they can't.

5 Look and write.

1 Can Emma swim?
   Yes, she can.

2 Can Emma rollerblade?
   ....

3 Can Fred rollerblade?
   ....

4 Can Fred swim?
   ....

5 Can Mary and Bob swim?
   ....

6 Can Mary and Bob rollerblade?
   ....

(6) **Write in the correct order.**

1 Can / ride bicycles? / they   Can they ride bicycles?

2 She / swim. / can't

3 climb trees. / Monkeys / can

4 you / Can / sing?

Let's Sing 🔘 Track 31

Listen and write. Then match.

jump   clap   ~~climb~~   swim   count   ride

Look, look, look at me.
I can (**1**) climb a tree. e
I can read and I can write.
I can (**2**) .... a bike. ....

Look, look, look at me.
I can (**3**) .... in the sea. ....
I can (**4**) .... up
very high. ....
I can touch the sky.

Look, look, look at me.
I can (**5**) .... to three. ....
I can (**6**) .... and
turn around. ....
I can touch the ground.

Fun Grammar Review

1 Listen and draw lines.  Track 32

2 Put a ✓ or a ✗.

1 There is a playground. ✓   **2** There is a bus. ....

3 There are two trees. ....   **4** There is a school. ....

5 There are lots of children. .... **6** There is a river. ....

3 Write.

1 She ....can swim..... .

2 He ....

3 They ....

4 It ....

5 He ....

6 She ....

4 Write about you.

1 Can you ride a bike? ....

2 Can you do a handstand? ....

3 Can you swim? ....

4 Can you sing? ....

5 Can you fly? ....

My English

Write about you and your friend.

I can swim. I can't fly. My friend can play football. He can't rollerblade.

I ....

My friend ....

Now draw a face.

I like milk.

I don't like oranges.

Track 33

We use the present simple to talk about facts. We make the present simple with I, you, we and they and the main verb: like, run, etc.

Affirmative	**Negative**	
	Long forms	**Short forms**
I like	I do not like	I don't like
You like	You do not like	You don't like
We like	We do not like	We don't like
They like	They do not like	They don't like

1 **Circle.**

1 I like / don't like eggs.

2 I like / don't like chicken.

3 We like / don't like honey.

4 We like / don't like milk.

5 They like / don't like breakfast.

6 They like / don't like oranges.

2 Match.

1 I ....like........ bread.
I don't like eggs.

2 I like oranges.
I .... salad.

3 I don't like milk.
I .... soup.

4 I .... chicken.
I like honey.

a ✗ ✓
b ✓ ✗
c ✓ ✗
d ✗ ✓

3 Match and write about you.

I like pizza.

Yes/No questions: *Do you like ...?*

Do you like honey?

Yes, I do.

Track 34

We use Do to make questions in the present simple with I, you, we and they.

Questions	Short answers
Do you like ...?	Yes, I do./No, I don't.
Do you like ...?	Yes, we do./No, we don't.
Do they like ...?	Yes, they do./No, they don't.

4 Circle about you. Then draw.

1 Do you like apples?   Yes, I do. / No, I don't.

2 Do you like bananas?   Yes, I do. / No, I don't.

3 Do you like pizza?   Yes, I do. / No, I don't.

4 Do you like oranges?   Yes, I do. / No, I don't.

      My favourite food

5 Choose and write.

don't (x2)   like (x2)   Do   do

1 Do you __like__ eggs?   Yes, I do.

2 _____ you like soup?   No, I don't.

3 Do you like chicken?   Yes, we _____ .

4 Do you like fish?   No, I _____ .

5 Do they _____ cakes?   Yes, they do.

6 Do you like bread?   No, we _____ .

6 Write and answer about you.

1 Do you like __chicken__ ?      _____

2 Do you like _____ ?   _____

3 Do you like _____ ?   _____

4 Do you like _____ ?   _____

Let's Chat   Track 35

Do you like fish, Patty?

Yes, I do!

7 Affirmative: *He/She/It*

> He gets up at seven o'clock.

 Track 36

We also use the present simple to talk about things we do regularly. To make the present simple with he, she and it, we add -s to the main verb.

He swims every day.
She rides her bike every day.
It gets up at seven o'clock.

Remember some verbs are different.

I do → He does
I go → She goes
I have → It has

7 Circle.

1 He ...... to school every day.
  a go   **(b)** goes

3 She ...... basketball at six o'clock every day.
  a play   **b** plays

5 ...... swim every day.
  a She   **b** They

2 ...... cleans his teeth at eight o'clock.
  a He   **b** I

4 He ...... breakfast at seven o'clock.
  a has   **b** have

6 We ...... our bikes every day.
  a ride   **b** rides

8 Match.

1 George gets up at seven o' clock.

2 Sarah has breakfast at eight o'clock.

3 Paul cleans his teeth every day.

4 Fiona goes to school at eight o'clock.

a

b

c

d

9 Write.

1

He plays with his ball every day.

2

....

3

....

4

....

5

....

6

....

7 Yes/No questions: *Does he swim everyday?*

Does he play **basketball** every day?

Yes, he does.

Track 37

We use Does to make questions in the present simple with he, she, and it.

Questions

Does he swim every day?
Does she run every day?
Does it have breakfast at seven o'clock?

Short answers

Yes, he does./No, he doesn't.
Yes, she does./No, she doesn't.
Yes, it does./No, it doesn't.

When we make questions with Does, we use the main verb.

Does he go to school every day? ✓   ~~Does he goes to school every day?~~ ✗
Does she like fish? ✓   ~~Does she likes fish?~~ ✗

10 Circle.

1 Does Tina read a book every day?
   a No, it doesn't.   **(b)** No, she doesn't.

2 Does Tom do his homework every day?
   a Yes, he does.   **b** No, I don't.

3 Does Bob play tennis every day?
   a Yes, they do.   **b** No, he doesn't.

4 Does Maria swim every day?
   a Yes, it does.   **b** No, she doesn't.

5 Does Sue go to school every day?
   a Yes, she does.   **b** Yes, I do.

6 Does Kim have breakfast every day?
   a Yes, she does.   **b** No, it doesn't.

11 **Write.**

1

Mark / do / his / homework / on Sunday?
Does Mark do his homework on Sunday?
No, he doesn't.

2

Tania / walk / to / school / on Monday?

....

....

3

Sam / play / basketball / on Friday?

....

....

4

Helen / rollerblade / on Wednesday morning?

....

....

Let's Sing 🔘 Track 38

**Listen and put in the correct order.
Then sing and dance.**

I see my friends and we all play, ...
Every day at three o'clock, 1
In my favourite zoo. ....
I come to the zoo. ....

They love me and I love them. ....
Chatter and Trumpet, ...
Karla and Tag, ...
We all love our zoo. ....
Patty and Sally too. ....

Fun Grammar Review ⑤

1 Write about you.

1 Do you get up at seven o'clock? ....

2 Do you go to school every day? ....

3 Do you like salad? ....

4 Do you play basketball on Sunday? ....

5 Do you have breakfast every day? ....

2 Look and write.

This is Sarah. She (1)  ....gets up............ at seven o'clock every day.

 She (2) .... and she cleans her teeth.

 She (3) .... to school at eight o'clock. At four o'clock she

 comes home and she (4) .... her ....

 She (5) .... at six o'clock.

At nine o'clock she (6)  .... her teeth.

3 Look and write.

		Monday	Tuesday	Wednesday	Thursday	Friday	Saturday	Sunday
1							☺	☺
2		☺	☺	☺	☺	☺	☺	☺
3			☺				☺	
4		☺	☺	☺	☺	☺	☺	☺
5		☺	☺	☺	☺	☺	☺	☺

1 Does he ride his bike every day?   *No, he doesn't.*

2 Does he play the guitar every day?   ....

3 Does she swim every day?   ....

4 Does she skip every day?   ....

5 Do they rollerblade every day?   ....

My English

Write about you and your friend.

I have breakfast at eight o'clock every day. I play football on Sunday. My friend
has a shower at seven o'clock every day. She goes to the zoo on Sunday.

I ....

....

My friend ....

....

Now draw a face.

8 Present continuous: affirmative

They're having a shower.

 Track 39

We use the present continuous to talk about something that is happening now.
We make the present continuous with am, are, is + a verb with -ing.

Long forms	**Short forms**
I am reading.	I'm reading.
You are reading.	You're reading.
He is reading.	He's reading.
She is reading.	She's reading.
It is reading.	It's reading.
We are reading.	We're reading.
You are reading.	You're reading.
They are reading.	They're reading.

When the verb ends in -e, we drop the -e and add -ing.

   hide + ing ➔ hiding   ride + ing ➔ riding

When the verb ends with a vowel and a consonant (swim), we sometimes double the consonant and add -ing.

   swim + ing ➔ swimming   run + ing ➔ running

1 **Match.**

1 He's sleeping.

2 She's doing her homework.

3 They're wearing pink dresses.

4 It's playing with a ball.

5 We're wearing green trousers.

a

b

c

d

e

2 **Circle.**

1 He ...... reading a book.
   a 's   **b** 're

2 We ...... playing a game.
   a 's   **b** 're

3 They ...... hiding.
   a 's   **b** 're

4 It ...... swimming.
   a 's   **b** 're

5 She ...... wearing a green skirt.
   a 's   **b** 're

6 I ...... reading a book.
   a 'm   **b** 're

8 Affirmative

3 Look and write.

1 They're ...climbing... a tree.

2 They're .... T-shirts.

3 He's .... a guitar.

4 She's ....

4 Write.

1 I .'m doing....................... (do) my homework.

2 He .... (write) a card.

3 She .... (read) a book.

4 They .... (play) a game.

5 You .... (hide) in the cupboard!

6 It .... (run).

(5) Write.

1

......He's wearing...... brown ...... trousers ......
and an orange ......sweater...... .

2

.... green
.... , yellow
.... and
red ....

3

.... a pink
....

4

.... a blue
.... and a
yellow ....

Let's Play

You're doing your homework!

8 Negative

I'm not playing football.

Track 40

Long forms	Short forms
I am not reading.	I'm not reading.
You are not reading.	You aren't reading.
He is not reading.	He isn't reading.
She is not reading.	She isn't reading.
It is not reading.	It isn't reading.
We are not reading.	We aren't reading.
You are not reading.	You aren't reading.
They are not reading.	They aren't reading.

6 Circle.

1 She ...... playing football.

   a isn't   **b** aren't

3 He ...... swimming.

   a aren't   **b** isn't

5 You ...... riding a bike.

   a aren't   **b** isn't

2 They ...... wearing skirts.

   a isn't   **b** aren't

4 I ...... singing.

   a 'm not   **b** aren't

6 It ...... sleeping.

   a isn't   **b** aren't

7 Write.

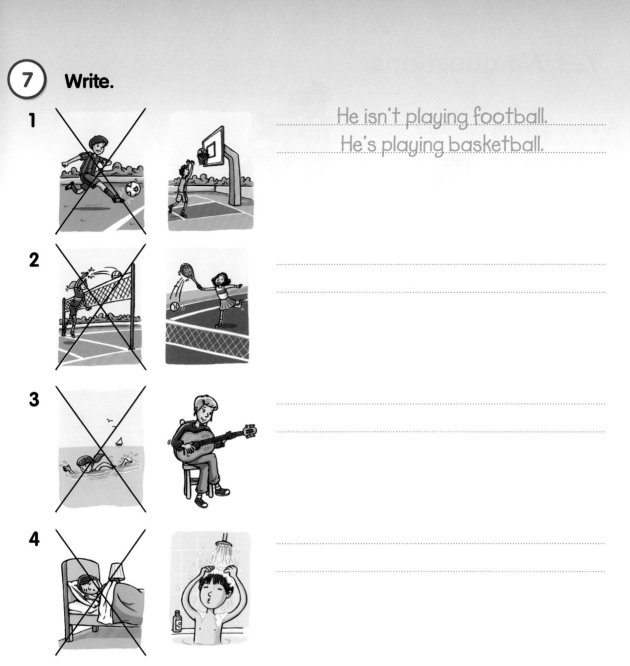

1 He isn't playing football.
He's playing basketball.

2

3

4

Let's Chat Track 41

We aren't playing volleyball. We're tired.

Yes/No questions

Are you playing football?

No, I'm not.

Track 42

Questions	Short answers
Am I reading?	Yes, you are./No, you aren't.
Are you reading?	Yes, I am./No, I'm not.
Is he reading?	Yes, he is./No, he isn't.
Is she reading?	Yes, she is./No, she isn't.
Is it reading?	Yes, it is./No, it isn't.
Are we reading?	Yes, you are./No, you aren't.
Are you reading?	Yes, we are./No, we aren't.
Are they reading?	Yes, they are./No, they aren't.

8 Circle.

1 ...... eating an apple?

   a Is he   **b** We are

3 ...... roaring?

   a He is   **b** Is it

5 ...... wearing a dress?

   a Is she   **b** It is

2 ...... coming?

   a She is   **b** Are they

4 ...... sleeping?

   a You are   **b** Are you

6 ...... snoring?

   a Is he   **b** She is

(9) Write.

1 Is she drinking?
..........Yes, she is...........

2  Are you hiding?

....

3  Is he eating?

....

4  Is it running?

....

5  Are they riding a bike?

....

6  Is he sleeping?

....

Let's Sing
Track 43

Listen and write.

are they   Are you   ~~dreaming~~   roaring   writing   is coming

Are they sleeping?
Are they (**1**) dreaming ?
Where are the animals
What (**2**) .... doing?
Are they reading?
Are they (**3**) .... ?
What is that terrible noise?

Are you eating?
Are you drinking?
Where are you, animals?
What are you doing?
(**4**) .... playing?
Are you hiding?
What is that terrible noise?

Hide all the toys!
Eat all the cake!
Jump into bed!
Sally (**5**) ....
upstairs!

We're not playing.
We're not eating.
Look at us, Sally,
We're very good animals.
Tag's not (**6**) ....
Trumpet's snoring.
That is the terrible noise!

Fun Grammar Review

6

1 Write yes or no.

1

Tag is playing basketball. __yes__

2

Karla is swimming. ....

3

Chatter is playing football. ....

4

Patty is sleeping. ....

2 Write.

1 She ___isn't swimming___ (not/swim).
She ___'s running___ (run).

2 He .... (not/roar).
He .... (snore).

3 You .... (not/wear) skirts.
You .... (wear) dresses.

4 It .... (not/sing).
It .... (fly).

3 Circle.

1 Tom _____ wearing brown trousers.
   a is   **b** aren't   **c** are

2 _____ they drinking?
   a Is   **b** Are   **c** Isn't

3 The girls _____ playing tennis.
   a isn't   **b** are   **c** am

4 She _____ swimming.
   a isn't   **b** am   **c** are

5 Mum and Dad _____ sleeping.
   a aren't   **b** 's   **c** 'm not

6 _____ he hiding?
   a Am   **b** Are   **c** Is

4 Read and answer.

The children are playing in the park. There are three boys and three girls. Bob is wearing a blue sweater. He is playing basketball. Tom and Joe are wearing yellow T-shirts. They're playing football. Mary is playing tennis with Tina and little Helen is playing with a water pistol. There is a big dog under a tree. It's sleeping.

1 Is Bob wearing a blue sweater?
   _____Yes, he is._____

2 Are Tom and Joe playing football?
   _____

3 Is Joe wearing a green T-shirt?
   _____

4 Is Mary playing tennis?
   _____

5 Is Helen hiding?
   _____

6 Is the dog playing with a ball?
   _____

My English

Write about you and your friend.

I'm doing my homework. I'm not sleeping.
My friend is playing tennis.
She isn't swimming.

I _____ .
My friend _____ .

Now draw a face.

9 This is/These are ...

This is my new bike.

These are presents.

Track 44

We use This is and These are to talk about things that are near. We use This is with a singular noun. We use These are with a plural noun.

① **Write** This **or** These.

1 This is a dolphin.

2 .... are girls.

3 .... are my books.

4 .... is my camera.

5 .... are crabs.

6 .... is my new sweater.

2 Write.

1  .... These are mobile phones. ....

2 ....

3  ....

4  ....

5  ....

Let's Sing 🔘 Track 45

Listen and circle.

(**1**) This is / These are a fish.
It's swimming in the sea.
I can see the (**2**) fish / crabs
And it can see me.
It can see me.

(**3**) These are / This is dolphins.
They're swimming in the (**4**) sea / river.
I can see the (**5**) dolphins / turtles
And they can see me.
They can see me.

10 Irregular plurals

They're people.

To make the plural of most nouns, we add -s at the end of the word.

book → books   cat → cats

To make the plural of many words that end with -x, -s, -ss, -ch, -sh and -o, we add -es.

box → boxes   dress → dresses
bus → buses   watch → watches

To make the plural of words that end with -y, we drop the -y and add -ies.

baby → babies   spy → spies

Irregular nouns change in different ways in the plural. Some irregular nouns don't change.

child → children   foot → feet
man → men   tooth → teeth
woman → women   fish → fish
person → people

1 Match.

1 fox — c
2 bus
3 family
4 foot
5 dress
6 person

a dresses
b people
c foxes
d families
e buses
f feet

2 Write.

1 I can see two .... spies ....

2 There are three .... in the park.

3 He has got two big ....

4 The .... have got bags.

5 The .... are wearing shirts.

6 The baby has got two ....

Let's Chat Track 47

This is an octopus.
These are crabs.

Track 48

Questions	Short answers
Is there …?	Yes, there is./No, there isn't.
Are there …?	Yes, there are./No, there aren't.

We use some with affirmative sentences. We use any with negative sentences and questions.

> Is there any chocolate? Yes, there is some chocolate./No, there isn't any chocolate.

1 Circle.

1 There are ...... bananas.
   a some   **b** any

2 There are ...... sweets.
   a some   **b** any

3 There aren't ...... crabs.
   a some   **b** any

4 There are ...... fish.
   a some   **b** any

5 Are there ...... stickers?
   a some   **b** any

6 There aren't ...... dolphins.
   a some   **b** any

2 Look and write A or B.

A

B

1 There aren't any carrots. A

3 There is a bowl. ....

5 There aren't any apples. ....

2 There are some sweets. ....

4 There isn't any chocolate. ....

6 There aren't any cherries. ....

3 Write. Use *some* **or** *any*.

1 .... There are some sweets. ....

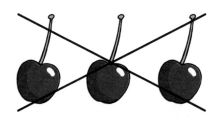

2 .... There aren't any cherries. ....

3 ....

4 ....

5 ....

6 ....

11 *some/any*

4 Write Are **or** Is. **Then answer.**

1 ...Are... there any cherries?
Yes, ...there are... .

2 .... there any sweets?
Yes, ...

3 .... there an apple?
Yes, ...

4 .... there a carrot?
No, ...

5 .... there any books?
No, ...

6 .... there any radios?
No, ...

Let's Sing

 Track 49

Listen and write.

cherries   bowl   any   carrots   ~~some~~   shelf   chocolates   sweets

There are (**1**) ...some... apples in the bowl.
There are some (**2**) .... in the drawer.
There are some bananas on the (**3**) ....
But we're looking for the **Secret Store**!

Are there (**4**) .... cherries?
Are there any sweets?
Are there any (**5**) .... ?
Are there any treats?

There aren't any cherries in the (**6**) ....
There aren't any (**7**) .... in the drawer.
There aren't any chocolates on the shelf.
But here it is, the **Secret Store**!

There are lots of (**8**) ....
There are lots of sweets.
There are lots of chocolates.
There are lots of treats.

12 Wh– questions:
What, Who, Where, How many?

Track 50

We always put question words at the beginning of a question.

What are they? They're presents.
Who has got a car? Dad's got a car.
Where are the children? They're in the bedroom.
How many sweets are there? There are ten.

We use the question form of the verb after question words.

What is it? ✓   ~~What it is?~~ ✗
Where are they? ✓   ~~Where they are?~~ ✗

① **Circle.**

1 ...... are you doing?
  a Who   **b** Where   **c** What

2 ...... stickers have you got?
  a Where   **b** How many **c** What

3 ...... is my book?
  a Where **b** How many **c** Who

4 ...... has the chocolate?
  a How many **b** Where   **c** Who

5 ...... is your friend?
  a What **b** Who   **c** How many

6 ...... is your school?
  a Who   **b** How many **c** Where

12 Wh– questions

2 Match.

1 Where is Sally?
2 Who has got the crayons?
3 What is your favourite animal?
4 How many cherries are there?
5 Where are the children?

a Sam has got the crayons.
b There are twenty cherries.
c They are in the park.
d She's in the river.
e Kangaroos.

3 Read and write.

1 _____What_____ are they? They're bikes.
2 _____ are they? They're in the playground.
3 _____ has got the bikes? Tag and Chatter have got the bikes.
4 _____ bikes are there? There are two.
5 _____ is the mobile phone? It's on the desk.
6 _____ is she doing? She's doing her homework.

4 Write.

1 _____Where are Tom and Ben?_____
Tom and Ben are **in the kitchen**.

2 _____
My favourite colour is **blue**.

3 _____
He has got **two computer games**.

4 _____
She's eating an **apple**.

5 _____
Her shoes are **under the bed**.

6 _____
There are **lots of bananas**.

1 What's he wearing?
He's wearing trousers.

2 Who is reading?

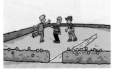

3 Where are the children?

4 How many bags are there?

5 What are they?

6 What is the lion doing?

Let's Play

Colour.

Fun Grammar Review (7)

1 Write.

1 .....What..... are the children doing?
They're playing.

2 .... are the children?
They're in the park.

3 .... babies are there?
There's one baby.

4 .... is drinking?
The baby is drinking.

5 .... is the dog doing?
It's sleeping.

2 Match.

16
10   twelve   11
eleven
twenty   thirteen   20
13
12   sixteen
ten

3 Write.

1 bus   .....buses.....   2 tooth   ....

3 dress   ....   4 butterfly   ....

5 woman   ....   6 watch   ....

4 **Write** This is **or** These are.

1 _____This is_____ a camera.

2 _____ sweets.

3 _____ a blue T-shirt.

4 _____ a shelf.

5 _____ biscuits.

5 **Write** some **or** any.

1 There aren't ...any... chocolates in the drawer.

2 There are _____ books on the shelf.

3 Are there _____ cars under the bed?

4 There aren't _____ pens in the bag.

5 Are there _____ chairs in the classroom?

My English

Write and draw. Then colour.

There is a banana in the bowl, but there isn't any chocolate. There are some cherries, but there aren't any sweets.

There is _____ .

_____

There are _____ .

_____

Now draw a face.

I can do this! 1

1 **Listen and colour.**  Track 51

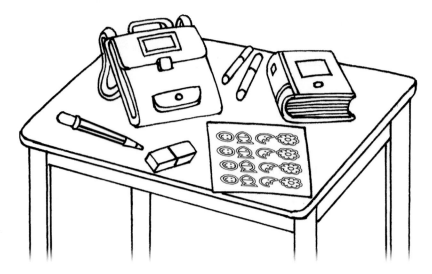

2 **Choose and write.**

~~flower~~   cat   elephant   dog   apple   fox   octopus   umbrella

a   flower ....

....

....

....

an   ....

....

....

....

3 **Put a ✓ or a ✗.**

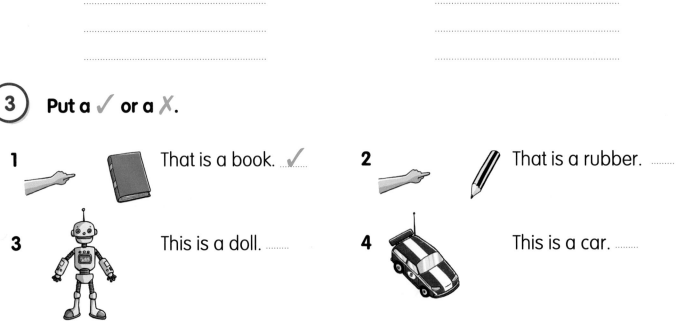

1   That is a book. ✓

2   That is a rubber. ....

3   This is a doll. ....

4   This is a car. ....

4 Write.

1 What's this?

It's a ball.

2 What's this?

....

3 What are they?

....

4 What are they?

....

5 Choose and write.

is   am   are (x2)   Is   Are

1 They ....are.... clowns.

2 .... he a pirate?

3 .... you a girl?

4 They .... friends.

5 She .... my sister.

6 I .... a boy.

6 Read and answer.

1 Are they pirates?   Yes, ...they are...... .

2 Are they friends?   No, ...

3 Is he your grandpa?   No, ...

4 Is she a dancer?   Yes, ...

5 Is it a monkey?   Yes, ...

6 Are you a boy?   ....

Hooray!

Draw and colour.

I can do this!

I can do this! 2

(1) **Listen and draw lines.**  Track 52

(2) **Circle.**

1 .... a bed.
    (a) There's   **b** There are

2 .... two bikes.
    a There's   **b** There are

3 .... lots of toys.
    a There's   **b** There are

4 .... a new train.
    a There's   **b** There are

(3) **Write** his, her **or** their.

1 She's got a bed.
   It's ....her.... bed.

2 They've got a prize.
   It's .... prize.

3 He's got a computer.
   It's .... computer.

4 She's got a desk.
   It's .... desk.

4 **Unscramble and write.**

1 He ...has... got ...arms... . samr

2 They .... got two .... tefe

3 She .... got brown .... riah

4 I .... got small .... raes

5 **Write** can **or** can't.

1 Monkeys ...can... climb.

2 Bears .... rollerblade.

3 Elephants .... fly.

4 Kangaroos .... jump.

5 Tigers .... run fast.

6 Goats .... sing.

6 **Write.**

1  .... He gets up .... at seven o'clock.

2 .... every day.

3 .... every day.

4 .... at eight o'clock.

Hooray!

Draw and colour.

I can do this!

I can do this! 3

1 **Listen and circle.**  Track 53

1 a  **b**    **2** a  b

3 a  b    **4** a  b

2 **Write** yes **or** no.

1 The boys are playing with the water pistols.   ....yes....

2 A girl is riding her bike.   ....

3 Two women are walking.   ....

4 A boy is playing basketball.   ....

5 Two monkeys are sleeping.   ....

3 Match.

1 Who is your friend?
2 Where is my camera?
3 What is he eating?
4 How many children are there?
5 Who is wearing a skirt?

a There are twenty children.
b Patty.
c It's on the shelf.
d Bob.
e Chicken and salad.

4 Write.

1

We're carrying presents.

2

3

4

5 Choose and write.

There is (x2)   There are   any (x2)   some

1 __There is__ a bowl.
2 Are there _____ crayons?
3 There aren't _____ carrots.
4 _____ a banana.
5 There are _____ apples.
6 _____ some cherries.

Hooray!

Draw and colour.

I can do this!

Look what I can do!

1 **Listen and write.**  Track 54

1 What's the name of the boy? _____Nick_____

2 How many children are there in his class?

_____

3 What's the name of the girl? _____

4 How many stickers has she got? _____

2 **Put a ✓ or a ✗.**

1  This is a crab. ✓

2  This is an apple. _____

3  This is a treehouse. _____

4  This is a shark. _____

5  This is a turtle. _____

6  This is a robot. _____

3 Unscramble and write.

1
k i t e
tike

2
_ _ _ _ _ _ _ _ _ _ _
llerbladsore

3
_ _ _ _ _
idora

4
_ _ _ _
ysot

5
_ _ _ _
keib

6
_ _ _ _ _
nairt

4 Write.

1 She gets up at seven o' clock.

2 ....

3 ....

4 ....

Look what I can do!

5 **Write about you.**

What do you do every day?

1 ....

2 ....

3 ....

4 ....

5 ....

6 ....

6 **Write about you.**

1 What's your name? ....

2 Have you got a dog? ....

3 Can you ride a bike? ....

4 Can you swim? ....

5 What are you wearing? ....

6 Do you like chocolate? ....

7 **Find the days and circle.**

O	V	W	T	F	G	A	E	L	P	T
N	E	C	M	S	B	D	M	I	Z	H
F	P	T	A	G	E	R	O	T	V	U
H	S	U	T	R	B	K	N	Y	S	R
O	W	E	D	N	E	S	D	A	Y	S
S	A	S	M	Y	P	X	A	E	P	D
U	F	D	L	W	R	O	Y	A	D	A
N	V	A	X	F	R	I	D	A	Y	Y
D	B	Y	U	M	L	I	K	N	C	E
A	N	P	S	A	T	U	R	D	A	Y
Y	O	K	T	R	P	F	O	Y	S	V

Hooray!

Draw and colour.

I can do this!

Pearson Education Limited
Edinburgh Gate
Harlow
Essex CM20 2JE
England
and Associated Companies throughout the world.

www.pearsonelt.com

First published 2010
Eleventh impression 2021

ISBN: 978-1-4082-4974-1

Printed in Slovakia by Neografia

Set in VagRounded

Publishing management by: hyphen

Illustrated by: GS Animation/Grupa Smacznego,
Christos Skaltsas/eyescream,
Eclipse Gráfica Creativa
Digital illustrations by: HL Studios, Long Hanborough, Oxford